Fauxccasional Poems

Other books by Daniel Scott Tysdal

The Mourner's Book of Albums

*Predicting the Next Big Advertising Breakthrough
Using a Potentially Dangerous Method*

The Writing Moment: A Practical Guide to Creating Poems

FAUXCCASIONAL POEMS

DANIEL SCOTT TYSDAL

icehouse poetry
an imprint of Goose Lane Editions

Copyright © 2015 by Daniel Scott Tysdal.

All rights reserved. No part of this work may be reproduced or used in any form or by any means, electronic or mechanical, including photocopying, recording, or any retrieval system, without the prior written permission of the publisher or a licence from the Canadian Copyright Licensing Agency (Access Copyright). To contact Access Copyright, visit www.accesscopyright.ca or call 1-800-893-5777.

Edited by Dani Couture.
Cover and page design by Chris Tompkins.
Cover photos: Kermit the Frog image taken from www.wikimedia.org (Edited by Designer), Oscar image taken from www.wikimedia.org (Edited by Designer), Dolphin image by Ross Hawkes (www.flickr.com/photos/rosshawkes) (Edited by Designer), Bible image by Amy Allcock (www.flickr.com/photos/amyallcock), Preacher image by niccolo2410 (www.flickr.com/photos/niccolo2410). All images from Flickr used under the guidelines of Creative Commons License 2.0 (creativecommons.org/licenses/by/2.0)
Printed in Canada.
10 9 8 7 6 5 4 3 2 1

Library and Archives Canada Cataloguing in Publication

Tysdal, Daniel Scott, 1978-, author
     Fauxccasional poems / Daniel Scott Tysdal.

Issued in print and electronic formats.
ISBN 978-0-86492-872-6 (pbk.).—ISBN 978-0-86492-821-4 (epub).—
ISBN 978-0-86492-845-0 (mobi)

     I. Title.

PS8639.Y84F38 2015   C811'.6   C2015-902835-3
                                           C2015-902836-1

We acknowledge the generous support of the Government of Canada, the Canada Council for the Arts, and the Government of New Brunswick.

Nous reconnaissons l'appui généreux du gouvernement du Canada, du Conseil des arts du Canada, et du gouvernement du Nouveau-Brunswick.

Goose Lane Editions
500 Beaverbrook Court, Suite 330
Fredericton, New Brunswick
CANADA E3B 5X4
www.gooselane.com

For Andrea.
What is constant in all the best possible worlds
is you and your work and your love.

Occasional poems are written to celebrate or memorialize a particular occasion, such as a birthday, a marriage, a death, a military engagement or victory, the dedication of a public building, or the opening performance of a play.

Fauxccasional poems are written to celebrate or memorialize a particular fake or speculative occasion, for example, the Iroquois landing on European shores in the 12th century or the Enola Gay's refusal to drop an atomic bomb on Hiroshima. Poems falsely attributed to real historical figures are also often considered fauxccasional.
— M.H. Abrams

Nothing that has never happened should be regarded as lost for history.
— Walter Benjamin

CONTENTS

YEAR 0-1945

Last Poem	11
New World	12
Sonnet 155	14
Burned at the Man	15
Chant d'amour pour l'Armée du Rhin	16
On Your Headcanon	18
War! War! War!	20
Bees Will Sing	21
Shame, a Paean	22
Addendum to "The Waste Land"	24
The Time Traveller's Pantoum	28
Horrorism	30
Wide Island	33

1946-2000

The Hand of Faith	37
Lo	41
Shell	42
Revolution (Tweetych)	43
Keep Our Country Clean!	44
The Discovery of Love, Excerpts from an Endless Oral History	46
Tell Me How	53
The Walls	54
What Will Happen to the Next Michael Jordan?	55
Imagine	57

Epithalamion	58
The Kermit Kingdom	60
01011001 00110010 01001011	61

2001 – YEAR 0

The Taliban Are the Most Famous Poets in America	65
Inside Job	67
The Messengers	69
Detroit City Meets the Invisible Hand	70
The King of Camelot	74
92,955,807 Miles	76
One More Love Poem	78
Fable Express	80
The Oath of Isis	82
I Wear a Hijab (Lol), or Professor Puts a Cupcake in the Fridge	83
Conch	85
The Correction Line	88
Last Poem	89
Notes	91
Acknowledgements	97

YEAR 0–1945

Last Poem

The remaining fragment of an ode ordered, Year 0, by the leadership of the First Philosopher King Republic.

    close the cave

  and shadows
        banish

Too far removed

Poets

     appearance

          a weapon

The waters

      well-ordered State.

New World

Examples of Iroquois influence on English writers following the Iroquois's 12th-century landing on European shores.

1. How Beoyote Lost Her Song

When Beoyote arrived in the world beyond the great waters, she discovered a war divided the land. Grendel, the monster of the woods, attacked the Scylding home of Heorot. The Scylding, the builders of this wood house, stormed the forest to hunt the beast. The way of this world was war.

Beoyote sang her song of unity to create a new world of the old one. She stopped the battle with her beautiful voice. Her melody showed the Scylding how their wood house was the same as Grendel's woods. The men, enrapt, agreed: all homes were homes. Yet, the men raged, the monster's skin divides it from us. Grendel also growled against her song: the wood house and the woods were united, but skin separated monster from man. The way of this world was war and the battle continued.

Beoyote was quick, though, and she halted the war again with her melody. This time her song taught the Scyldings and Grendel that skin was skin. Both men and monster agreed, but the way of this world remained war. Words divided, both sides cried as they prepared to return to battle. Before they could, Beoyote stopped them again with her song. All words were words, she sang. The men were the monster and the monster was the men. The war stopped as all divisions vanished. The former combatants slumbered as one at peace.

Just as Beoyote peeled away the boundaries of her home, skin, and words to join them in this new world, she watched the old war and world begin again. From the dreams of these sleeping beings, Grendel arose roaring and the Scyldings, armed, rose up to meet the beast in battle. Beoyote sang her song to the dreamed monster and dreamed men, teaching the lesson of unity: all homes were homes, all skin was skin, and all words were words. These dreamed beings, like their dreamers, united in sleep, but they too dreamed the old war and world back to life.

This cycle continued. Beoyote taught the dreamed combatants the sleep of peace and the sleeping beings birthed the war again in their dreams. She sang her song again and again and again until she could no longer sing it, her beautiful voice reduced to a plaintive howl.

This is how Beoyote lost her song. And yet this is also why she still ventures out at night to cry into the dark. For even though she can no longer sing, she still hopes she can, howling, strike a note that shows us we are the creators of the lines that divide us and we have the power to sing them into new uniting forms.

2. Excerpt from *The Canterbury Tales* (manuscript dated 1390), "The General Prologue" (Lines 1-18)

Here begins the Book of the Tales of Canterbury

When winter with his blizzard stark with cold
Has tied in ice the castle and the wold
And frozen all the grain that was not reaped
And cast the youthful year to aged sleep;
When from this icy land no Iroquois
Build New World fire to offer heat to thaw
That deeper cold that men beget to tear
Men from all things, like voice cut off from air;
Then wakes the call, so true, of the Great Spirit
For we who in this silence need to hear it
And rise in hope to balance out our rage
And undertake our veiled pilgrimage.
Of England, we to Canterbury wend,
Though Christian love is not our final end;
We quest to praise the people this love martyred,
Their lack the land we seed with our true ardour:
This woman ripe with sky who fell in birth,
Now from her riven body grows our earth.

Sonnet 155

Composed on the occasion of the publication of Dr. Marjorie Rubright's Not to Be: How One Forgotten Man Made the Globe. *Oxford: OUP, 2014.*

One ray of light does not the dark curtail.
No hunger's fed by apricots alone.
A solitary wolf's predation fails
to carve a path. The body's more than bone.
Yet Rubright claims a candle is a sun,
asserting Globe's Grand Players did not write
their ageless plays and poems; Shakespeare's the one.
She bids our bard collective a lone good night.
Or does she wake us to a truer flaw?
Our grasp of authorship was far too cramped:
a sonnet's lines by lover's eyes are drawn,
by royals, stars, and blood the plays are stamped
  and sing, "*totus mundus agit* art;
  in each great work we all compose a part."

Burned at the Man

Composed on the occasion of the opening of the Salem Wood Trials Memorial Forest, formerly Forest River Park. This poem was placed on a plaque at the memorial's entrance when the memorial opened in 1993, three centuries after the trials ended.

Remember the pain the wood fed:
the cattle the fiendishly twisting fence post
freed and the men who wound up poor.

Remember the blight the wood spread:
the fields the cruelly curving hoe
killed and the women who starved.

Remember the sickness the wood bred:
the cold the wickedly warping door jamb
welcomed and the children who died.

Remember the high men who saved us:
the men of cloth, law, and letters who
held the low wood still enough to burn.

Remember the good men who with this bad
wood burned, knowing they alone were
upright enough to serve as stakes in the fire.

Remember this wood and its warping
endure, and we must burn with the spirit
of sacrifice lit by these men, enflamed, in flames.

Chant d'amour pour l'Armée du Rhin

Modernized translation of a poem composed September 21, 1802, on the occasion of the tenth anniversary of the National Convention. The original was first published in Citizen de Sade's Poèmes pour la Révolution. *Paris: Libegalfra, 1805.*

Now everything's an orgy here so rise
and take your place amid the fleshy cloud,
and every set of lips you see, please soil
with clits and cocks and tongues — just rub and stick.
Your heart's a pen, the scene a blankened page,
when gluttons howl to what they nosh, "Now gorge!"

Our age renews all gods within this "gorge!"
Not flocks of birds but clusterfucks now rise:
full clusterfucks of crows, of doves. The page
turns too on bees — not swarms, but cum-filled clouds.
A herd's a gang. And "falls" for rain don't stick;
the rains, like drops from enemaed asses, soil.

Your skin for every seed now is a soil
as warm as bread, fresh-baked, and deep — a gorge
descenders find, descending, tight and stick
yet persevere: to deepen here's to rise.
An octopus, your heart hurls ink that clouds
hate's eyes with love, ordains lust's king your page.

My job's to catalogue upon this page
the bugs and blooms that populate our soil:
the androgyn whose nipples lactate clouds;
the man whose every pore's a puss to gorge
for she whose every hair, aroused, will rise,
erect, and penetrating please the stick-

sharp stare of eyes that, disembodied, stick
to staring's joys; the moans whose soundings page
elation in all ears; the piss whose rise
reveals in air orific sylphs; the soil-
like muck from which we sculpt these dolls to gorge
the puppet us, mirroring our cloud.

An ocean's not a depth without its cloud,
and yes not yes without the ayes that stick
inside the throat, too plump to heave or gorge,
and no's not no without its void: a page
as dark and small as specks of coal-charred soil.
There's more, and *more*, but more beyond must rise.

So cloud the words on every other page,
and stick with us, so close. We leap from soil
into this gorge in which to fall's to rise.

On Your Headcanon

Composed January 12, 2014, on the occasion of the fifth anniversary of the suicide of Blair Desi Smith. Dan Tysdal generated the poem using the ByronAIc Hero App, selecting as the persona Robert De Niro.

In your headcanon, your buddy Tysdal says, he
says that *Heat* don't end with a stock chase,
while Bickle falls taking out the Prez, see,
and Jake dies in the ring, demons erased.
And in your dreams I act just for Scorsese;
Casino is the final film I grace.
In your fan annals, I'm Best Actor twice,
concurring with Marty and taking the role of Christ.

Your dreams? Sting *me*? Yeah, sure, a little bit.
What fuckin' grinds? How such a faithful fan
could live my movies' pitch then swing and miss.
Each script you penned had roles for me to man,
and you and Tysdal tried to stage, no shit,
a high school *Taxi Driver*! Took balls. Got banned.
Yet, Blair, these lives I played, you never got 'em;
you swore to rise you first must hit rock bottom.

Rock bottom, Tysdal tells me, was your all —
in Avalon Apartments in Moose Jaw,
in phone calls from Fort Mac and Montreal,
as if to flee the jungle you must saw
the bridge in two, into the river fall,
and fester in the muck until you're raw.
This Russian Roulette? It's got a real bullet,
a trigger where a finger fits to pull it.

You never took a cannon to your head.
You slipped into the slower barrel of
a bottle, pills, and tub filled to the edge.
Does that make you the hero, kid? The tough
whose silence, drunk, recites, "The play is dead,
the thing of death's the thing, so give its rough
and savage bull this stage we can't invent
or ascertain. *That* is entertainment."

In Tysdal's headcanon you don't sink in that tub,
except on film, while playing a man who drowns.
To cheers, you thank him, Oscar raised way up,
then shout, "Hey, Tiz, Death couldn't knock me down."
You don't become this Betamax-like hub
of void that loops your shape with light and sound
in the television brain of your good friend.
You play on, and with that rocky base contend.

War! War! War!

Composed on the occasion of the second round of recruitment for Union battalion poets during the American Civil War. An original version of the poster is on display at the Gettysburg Museum and Visitor Center, and it is reproduced here in textual form with their permission.

Header Text: Patriots Your Country Needs You!

Mid-Upper Left Image: Eagle, gripping a sheaf of arrows and laurels in its talons, lifts in its beak a banner that reads, "The Union Forever!" Rays of light emanate from behind the eagle's outspread wings.

Mid-Lower Left Text: Active young poets wanted! / Able bodied and imaginative. / Replacement versifiers for 50 Union regiments.

Mid-Upper and Lower Right Text: Pen your poetry sample now! / 1. Rewrite the following stanza with patriotic zeal: / "I looked at something and saw this thing / and felt this sort of, kind of feeling / and now those famous symbol things / and something on our shared feeling." / 2. Form five metaphors for a cannon. 3. Fill in these blanks from the perspective of Confederate scum: "When I see the Union flag, I feel _____. I want to take the flag and _____." 4. Describe [picture of Abraham Lincoln]. 5. What is your favourite onomatopoeia for gunfire?

Footer Text: Bring your poetry sample to Head-Quarters at 1373 Broadway / Or, in the Evening at the Residence of Capt. Honstain, corner Leonard and Devoe Streets, Williamsburg. / Put Your Country's Future in Your Hands!

Bees Will Sing

Composed by Friedrich Engels in the fall of 1873, after news broke that Karl Marx was an agent provocateur employed and instructed by an international consortium of capitalists. There is no evidence to determine whether Engels wrote this poem before or after assassinating Marx, who was attempting to seek asylum in the United States.

This hoax pulled off by Marx, the pig,
does not change a thing: all radical singing
is still akin to the buzz of bees in a hive
improvised in the blowhole of a beached,
ocean-starved, and rotting sperm whale.
Men approach this leviathan with dynamite
to make it blow. Gulls, ravenous, circle.
Once, that whale fired through the sea
as wild and joyous as a heaven-aimed
bullet on a sun-pummelled victory day.
Once, that dynamite was a confederacy
of unallied planet-strewn elements.
Once, dynamite gestated undetected
in the word "power." It lingered unlit
in the electrical impulses of one man's
brain matter. If I bear your body from
the future, rotting like that whale's,
you must not turn away. It is history, bursting,
that will cast our forms into a swarm
whose drone blasts back. All singing *is*
is a bee. Don't look away. All singing is a bee.
Wrap your hand around yourself and sting.

Shame, a Paean

Dramatic monologue composed on the occasion of discovering a psychiatric evaluation undertaken five years back.

Has this ever happened to you? You're rushed
to "Emerg" and the psychiatrist on duty walks you
through this form to help her assess what sort
of shape you're in. She asks you to rate on a scale of 1
to 100 all sorts of things, I mean, you name it —
your anger, anxiety, depression. This happened
to me five years ago. I just found the form
while sorting through piles of junk in my office.
"Shame: 90" was what I wrote back then. I've already
filled three plastic bags with material to chuck. Cognitive
distortion was the diagnosis. What digits
for today do yesterday's augur? What numbers, I
wonder, would you mark on those scales — five
years ago, or today? Humour me: Anger
___, Anxiety ___, Depression ___. It'll help,
I swear. What is the word for that feeling
we must rate to get better? I swear. I need
your help. Give this word, or any like it,
a little ink: _____.

I know this is not the sort of poem I'm meant to make
(because not a word of it is false), but my friend Mat says
we're obliged to loom a poem from every thread
that reaches out to be a web. This is the one thing
we can do right. Try it. Shame: ____. What lines tender
their loose ends from the number you fit in that blank?
Take hold of them. I can wait. And don't worry
if you can't spin every strand into its geometric net.
Tangle the lines that snap and end half-spun in the pile
I've saved here: "_____,"
"when you crack an egg over a flame-sizzled
skillet, the ghost of the living bird that drops

by surprise to that fire is shame," "_____
_____," "cutters cut, starvers
stave off bites," "mixed-up mountain climbers
(lacking mountains, gear, an urge to rise) is not
a nice thing to call those of us who jump,"
"_____
_____," "distorters distorting distort."

Let's break the rules and remake this into a love poem
for any of you who need love. You could've been with us
in the woods when it happened. Love is shame's
other, the laughter to its shallow moan. Moh,
Katie, Safa, Kris, Mattieu, Faatima, and me (and you,
too (forget the facts), if you'll lend a hand
and add your name: _____) formed
a tiding of magpies in those woods, hunting
matter to nest on the limbs of our blank pages.
Other things we can do right: plan to write
the poems we are called to write, or plan
to plan for the sake of this fellowship. For reasons

we could not discern, someone who haunted
the woods before us had hammered a nail
into the bark of a tree in a clearing. The nail stuck
out like a friendly finger pointed in half-recognition
and we each agreed to write a piece for next week
to hang from it. Safa raised her phone to snap
the nail's picture, but the lens directed right at her
was active so that her face filled the screen
instead, and it seemed, briefly, that her features
had been carved onto the head of that nail.
I pointed this out, and the whole lot of us laughed
so damn hard, the shame now being we have no way
to hear your laughter or know what you will write
to hang from that nail, how you'll web this wonder
on the artifice of a page as clear as this line:

_____.

Addendum to "The Waste Land"

Composed by T.S. Eliot in April of 1926 on the occasion of the fifth anniversary of the first War of Art victory by "The Waste Land."

VI. The War of Art

The corpse sprouted. It healed the wound	
With a wound. The dead land wilted, now	435
Fertile with the dead. No more fishing	
For the sickly mended king. Wonders	
Are few, said he, yet of all things is Man	
The least Wonderful. Why did no old quest	
For the grail in rhyme or hide succeed?	440
The chalice, the clairvoyant answers	
(In a voice from the past we could not fiddle	
With until today), is in fact two chalices,	
Neither of which are visible until the seeker	
Sees that he must seek two cups: Peace	445
Without Peace and the unchanging Word	
That enforces it. Every great King	
Is the greatest clairvoyant; the rules	
He founds precisely rule.	
Every new desert	450
Our grails spring is divided into two shores.	
Beyond one shore swells the dry sea	
Of slaves, beyond the other thunders	
The unreal sea of actual exile.	
Never again will sweet voices cry to the sea foam,	455
κὤττι μοι μάλιστα θέλω γένεσθαι;	
Generals and jesters, united in time,	
Are united deeper still in the time it takes	
To feel the rhythm of this choice forced	
As dance is imposed on a hooked fish.	460
The chorus knows only one song:	

The men who opt for chains
Are free to forge our reign!
God save our Peace!
Those who choose exile's roam   465
Receive the golden dome
Of life without a home!
God save our Peace!

At most, the sea foam, the awful foam
Of these swallowing seas of unrooted rock   470
And rocky depths sounds in its swallowing
The melody that might have played the dream
Of an embracing shore, but formed nothing,
Which is better than throbbing as carrion,
Burning as a crab in its boiled water shell.   475
These nothings and these nothings are a beacon,
Sont un écho redit par mille labyrinthes;
C'est pour les coeurs mortels un divin opium!

If there were dreams to sell,
What would you buy? The dream   480
Of the chalices reburied in their dust.
The dream of this chalice stained
With the piss of avenging nymphs.
The mouth of this chalice carved
Into the living whiskey-ashed maw   485
Of a furious servant who cries
A true, endless portrait of the King,
With his diseased donkey for a cock
And ruined horses for emissions
And the ruin brought upon the wombs   490
Of all he mounts. I dream of teaching
This sick, true mouth to chant
Without end the spell that drowns
Our waste in the final flood
And shines on the seas we feed   495
The evaporating light of lights.

All my silver for this spell:
Pluvia deorsus, pluvia deorsus,
Pluvia deorsus in nobis,
Ex magna altitudo, 500
Ex magna altitudo.

Judge, the wrongly exonerated outlaw
Howls (guilty of making life a crime),
Reverse your verdict, salvage the ruins
Shored by these fragments, 505
This rhythmical grumbling;
Deliver all those we trespass against
From us, from the victorious loss
Of not being us in yet another losing win
For we who are what we have made 510
Of the world: a caged and wrinkled thing,
Prophetic, mean, rotting, and thirsty,
Shrivelled, and feeding, and unable to die.

Notes on "Addendum to 'The Waste Land'"

When the League of Nations ratified the War of Art Treaty on January 16, 1921, I, like so many, celebrated. Indeed, I had passionately argued in support of the treaty in our own British Parliament and to League members in Geneva. The War of Art Treaty promised an end to the brutal, inhuman violence of diseased trenches, bloodied barbed wire, and the deafening storm of artillery. Artists, not soldiers, would settle national quarrels. Ink would spill in place of blood. Competitions between Great Works of Art would halt forever the atrocities of Great Wars. Yet far from ushering in an era of international fellowship, the War of Art Treaty has bred a much crueller time. Thanks to victory after victory by my poem "The Waste Land," the British Empire now covers two thirds of the globe, and the people of each nation my poem defeats are faced with an impossible, inviolable choice: enter into servitude to the British crown or flee — to the diminishing, neighbouring lands or to the open, unclaimed sea. Thus, I add to the original poem this addendum, "VI. The War of Art," as a form of protest, sabotage, and, I suppose many will say, treason. I wish to stop my work from achieving yet another losing victory and to add my voice to the swelling chorus of those who demand the return of the sanity of war.

VI. The War of Art

Line 434. Cf. Hozai XIV, ii.
436. V. Weston: *From Ritual to Romance*; chapter on the Fisher King.
437. Cf. *Antigone*, 332-3:
"Wonders are many, yet of all
Things is Man the most wonderful."
447. Cf. Webster, *The White Devil*, III, vi:
"All murderers are oracles, you see,
Foretelling night for those they wake to night."
456. V. Sappho, "Hymn to Aphrodite."
462. I would be a fool not to take the opportunity to state definitively that, despite official statements asserting otherwise, I am not responsible for "God Save Our Peace." I may be the unwilling author of our Reign of Terror, but I am not the author of its unofficial anthem.
469. Cf. Stevens, "The Idea of Disorder at the Annexation of Key West":
"The sea is now their mask. No more are we
The makers of what is and is not song."
474. Phenomena which today are so common as to stand less as fabulistic correlatives and more as mimetic reproductions.
477. V. Charles Baudelaire, "The Beacons."
479. V. Thomas Beddoes, "Dream-Pedlary."
483. Cf. *A Midsummer Night's Dream*, V, i, 429.
488. Cf. Ezekiel XXIII, xx.
498. V. Severinus, *Ars Lugere*, II, 255-8.
503. Cf. *Anthos*, IV, iii:
"μιασμός ἀφαντόω βίος μιασμός."
511. V. Petronius: *Satyricon*; the Sibyl at Cumae.

The Time Traveller's Pantoum

Composed on the occasion of the birth of the first time traveller.

I've travelled to my start to save myself.
Myself at twenty-five first travelled time
To this the moment of my birth to stop
My newborn cry from ending my mom's breath.

Myself, at twenty-five, glows with his feat,
Though I, at fifty, know his triumph's cost.
Our mother breathes beyond our birth once more,
But more loss breeds beyond what we can save.

Though I, at fifty, know his triumph's cost,
I also know his drive to fix it all.
More loss breeds far beyond what we can save,
But he, like me before, will travel time

And also know this drive to fix it all —
To stop the Holocaust, Titanic's crash —
But he, like me before, will travel time
And learn that blazes snuffed are blazes spread.

To stop the Holocaust, Titanic's crash,
Means making new catastrophes arise,
Means learning blazes snuffed are blazes spread.
The wars you axe will gain another berth.

And making new catastrophes arise,
You age and lose the years you need to end
The wars that wax and gain and burn and birth
A panting beast you will not live to kill.

I've aged and lost the years I need to end
The tragedies that take our breath away.
A panting beast, I will not live; to kill
Eternal ruin one needs eternal lungs.

In tragedies that take our breath away
Find oxygen to raise the better self
Whose budding lungs we need to save from ruin —
The future we must dream and dreaming grasp.

In search of words to save my former self,
In this the moment of our birth, I stop.
An ancient me appears and crying gasps,
"I've travelled to my start to save myself."

Horrorism

Composed on the occasion of the seventy-fifth anniversary of the first Horrorist exhibition, September 1, 1939.

1.

No one noticed at first: that art had not
been real,
        that Horrorists had made
                              it
real.

    The *Mona Lisa* remained displayed
                          as though
she remained;
        Alain Riva's position selling
tickets at the Louvre was filled
                      when he missed,
for one
      week, every
                shift. The great Horrorist

2.

shift occurred on September 1, 1939. The exhibition
began with the arrival
                          at the Louvre
of this:
        a letter from Riva
        on a crate that contained
        the original *Mona Lisa*
        in her original frame with
        Riva's skinned face fixed
        to her face, one iconic eye

peeking through one of Riva's
empty, open
        lids. In his letter,

3.

    "The Horrorist Manifesto," Riva wrote,
"I am one brother of six who was not butchered
while committing butchery in the Great War." "I
have butchered myself," he wrote, "to begin
the butchering of all art whose only art is to lie."
"No more make-believe," he wrote. "No more
concealing the barbarism of art's concealment of
the barbarism of our kind." "The *Mona Lisa*," he
wrote, "that presently hangs on your liberated walls
is a perfect replica created from my corpse

4.

and my now liberated liberating soul."
        The *Riva Lisa*, as we,
        Riva's
        forbears,

know it now, now more iconic
        than the first,
        was destroyed,
        Da Vinci's original Lisa

returned to her place.
        Gallerygoers returned,
        though now to behold
        the aura of the horror

she replaced,
>> each visitor struggling
to imagine the twist
of the mouth that had

gaped
> toothless over
her mystifying
smile.

5.

Today,
> all art
>> is real. We face
the truth of horror. "Horror,"

as Riva wrote, "is art's only
> hygiene." "No more
belief in
make-believe."

Wide Island

Sestinaiku composed on the occasion of the seventieth anniversary of the Enola Gay's refusal to drop an atomic bomb on Hiroshima, Japan.

They were history's page:
guide the Enola Gay's rise
into and through clouds;
with Little Boy, stick
a radioactive gorge
in Japanese soil.

But they could not soil
Hiroshima's untouched page
with War's need to gorge,
War's desire to rise
each day with a bigger stick —
pound flesh into clouds.

Tibbets and crew, clouds
of War's fog cleared from eyes' soil,
saw — as with a stick
bug in trees, a page
stained in a tome — one foe's rise
don't mean slit the gorge

of all folks, or gorge
the forest with fiery clouds,
or to the shelf rise
and every book soil
with glue so every last page,
inseparable, sticks.

What of their "No" sticks?
Monuments like ice gorges
in time's sun. Pages
on traitor saints. Clouds
of lotus *kaiju* films; soil
for Heartzilla's rise

against War's dim rise.
Mostly, though, "Yes, sirs" bloom, stick-
ups of hope, scorched soil,
the old bastion's gorge
stocked with more weaponized clouds
to answer death's page.

Please rise, Peace, your page
rare, a walking stick of cloud,
soil borne from Love's gorge.

1946–2000

The Hand of Faith

Composed by Nicolas Cage in anticipation of the seventieth anniversary of the Golden Nugget Casino, which opened August 30, 1946. Excerpted from the email promoting the Golden Nugget's $1,000,000 Last Vegas Poetry Contest™.

i. The Hottest Bitch in the Room

You do want a lap dance tonight. God
is the hottest bitch in the room. Snap your
fingers and wave the c-note of your open
heart. This is not the God of the scriptures
or the spiritualists or the sects or, even,
the sexts. You do want a cigarette tonight.
Light it against the skin of this hot God.
This is the God who enfables patterns
from blank slate and the spangled webs
of neon blurred by a million squinting
eyes. Who do you think strobed your
roving robes? Who do you think made you
the second hottest bitch in this room?

ii. Nugget

Without hunger, who could tell
meat from flesh, flesh from sun,
or sun from the violin whose strings
are the rays of the same heat, its strum
the strains of the morning's envelopes
as they await the letters we write,
and those we leave unwritten, and those —
the crux — we write but do not send,
saving them for the envelope of night,
that final nugget of the bountiful rush
we've got no way of hauling out of town?

iii. Oasis

A voice cracks suddenly from a pitcher
of milk; from the breast leaks suddenly
mouths, an oasis of them, staining
the desert of the shirt, trickling down
the desert of the body, and pooling briefly
with palms, migrating birds, roaming
nomads, parched camels, and yawning
newborns at the desert of the feet
before evaporating into the oasis
of nothing that flourishes on the desert
of that original voice-cracked air.

iv. Nuggets

In the Middle Ages, a sect of disgraced knights
invented a bow that could only nock ice arrows
and could fire only when aimed directly at dirt
on sun-crushed days. Worms and buried enemies
were its chief game. It was their descendants who
gave us the game of chance played with stone tablets
the size of ten men. Rarely were more than three
hands completed. The goats that powered the dealing
mechanism died of exhaustion or one of the players
was flattened by what otherwise would have been
a winning hand. The mirror that returns bursts of
blinding light in place of reflections hangs in the hall
through which their ancestors, blindfolded, passed.
Today, their kin seek investors for a machine
that mines nuggets of minerals major industries
have yet to recognize as essential. They will come knocking
for your coin, just as you will go knocking for theirs.
Trust me. The prototype, though complete, is only capable
of mining the thought balloons that blossom muck-like
from the water penetrated heads of the victims
of the enduring deluge of arrows cut from ice.

v. Marquee

There is a superhero whose emblem
is a full-sized, fully functioning
casino, and whose mask is this casino's
thousand-plus room, zero vacancy
hotel. This much I know. I have discerned
the sounds of the slots, shuffled decks,
alcohol and mix-cracked ice,
the tearing away of sheets to beat sleep
or rise. What I've failed to uncover
is how this hero fought or who,
the nature and name of his mortal
enemy, or the face of the fiend
who killed him and dumped his corpse
here. Is this hero resurrectable
or truly gone? Is his death the delusion
of CEO-swayed editors or the de-lettered
marquee of an epoch's absolute end?

vi. The Nugget

The nugget, wrinkled and worn,
shuffles into the room with the aid
of its walker and gasps a nugget
of wisdom about nuggets and
the accrual of the minute, nuggets
and units and unity, a circling
and elliptical yarn that cuts short
as you grasp that you are, in truth,
hallucinating, staring not
at a walker-borne nugget but,
instead, at a bulb-less socket
that blooms in a garden of burnt out
bulbs, an hallucination that is itself
one obscure element among millions
in the dream of the monster who *was*

hiding under the bed, who *did*
eat the kids, and who is nothing more
than the chord no guitar ever played
because it was never that in or out
of tune, even as that other music started
and those other lights rose.

vii. The Mirage

There was the flower. We scorched
its petals, stem, and roots. Out of
the ash we erected the mirage of the flower.

There was the rock. We hammered
its surface, slants, and core. Out of
the dust we erected the mirage of the rock.

There was the height. We collapsed
its pull, lift, and view. Out of
the ruins we erected the mirage of the height.

We wait now for the ones who will catch sight
of our mirages and assemble from them
the new flower, the real rock, the true height.

Lo

Ballad composed on the occasion of the founding of the First Church of the Free Follower Fellowship.

A marionette, it's true, I am,
    but I pick my puppeteer;
a second set of strings runs from
    my heart to Master's ear.

I even chose my recent role:
    the fourth — the late — Magi.
The empty Manger in Act One
    I worship as God's Child.

Act Two begins and I sing songs
    to praise the Missing's balm.
Act Three I do the *Danse Absence*.
    Act Four's "The Follower's Psalm":

"I do not follow followers;
    I follow following.
The fallow path's within the path
    and flowers the fringes string."

Our routine done, my Master asks,
    "You're free. Why don't you leave?"
"If I wait here, the Second Coming
    will have to follow me."

Shell

Composed on the occasion of the Cuban Missile Crisis. Originally published in Marilyn Monroe's The Collected Works of Norma Jeane. *New York: Gaines, Kurtzman and Neuman, 1964.*

I do not know the parts of the bomb
or the parts of our mothers,
but what I do grasp is that both
hold both. The nervous nervous
system circuits the ignition-hitting
burst; the warhead, ignited, spreads
a brief womb over the city, amid
the city, birthing ruin, a conch
that calls forth the roar of drained
seas. The satellite, its vicious
vision, is derived from the pipes
whose installation plans I'm sketching
out. They'll take us straight to the basin
where dust is the blossom of every
single seed. Here's your shovel. Dig.

Revolution (Tweetych)

Tweets composed July 15, 1967, on the occasion of the tenth anniversary of Twitter.

@clearlyleary (Verified Account): Turn on, tune in, tweet out #twitrev

@therealcheguevara (Verified Account): Don't care if I fall as long as someone take up my acct and keeps tweeting. Free T 4 RT #twitterrevolution

@landslideLBJ (Verified Account): SMH Brezhnev says he and #ussr are world power. Then why refuse to join the #twitterrevolution

@psychedelicpearl: kk RT@droboogiebeatle: Twitter u bigger den us now and we biggr den Jesus ;) #twitrev

@revmlk (Verified Account): In the end we don't remember the tweets of enemies but the friends who don't favorite/RT #twitrev

@prezdegaulle (Verified Account): Vive le #twitter libre! Vive le twitter #français! Et vive la #france! #twitrev

@NationalNOW: @landslideLBJ how r u tweeting to bring #women into full participation in the twittersphere tmb #twitterrevolution

@thefamilyman: if u no no sense makes sense join our #tweetup: http://ow.ly/CdqKN #twitrev #twitterrevolution #twitter #revolution

@newordersuharto (Verified Account): hey @therealcheguevara and all u #commies why dont u follow me jk #twitterrevolution

@campbellsoup (Verified Account): In the future, every tweet will trend for 15 seconds. #twitrev

@chairmao (Verified Account): IMHO 2 read 2 many books is harmful. Let 100 tweets bloom! #twitterrevolution

Keep Our Country Clean!

Jingle composed to the tune of The Doors's "Light My Fire" to promote the launch of American Businesses for a Clean America's "Keep Our Country Clean!" campaign on April 22, 1970. Through the campaign, ABCA provided $100,000 (US) in arts funding to help "re-define clean in America," a funding pool that has increased annually.

You know that it's an ugly flaw
To think that beauty doesn't change.
What one age takes as natural law
Another understands as strange.
Come on, keep our country clean.
Come on, keep our country clean.
Try to fix our eyes to see.

Artists need to show us how
To cleanse our symbols, lore, and ways
Of all the filth the past endows
On what should be our bright new days.
Come on, keep our country clean.
Come on, keep our country clean.
Try to fix our eyes to see.

Waste is really neo-flowers
And smog's a sweater for the sky.
Radiation's one slick shower
And nerves go wild for pesticides.
Come on, keep our country clean.
Come on, keep our country clean.
Try to fix our eyes to see.

If you know you've got the skills
To clean up what we mean by clean,
To craft fine art from oil spills,
Then call up ABCA for some green.

Come on, keep our country clean.
Come on, keep our country clean.
Try to fix our eyes to see.
Try to fix our eyes to see.
Try to fix our eyes to see.
Try to fix our eyes to see.

The Discovery of Love, Excerpts from an Endless Oral History

Composed on the occasion of the publication of The Discovery of Love: An Oral History *(Toronto: UTP, 2009), which marked the thirtieth anniversary of the passing of the Gay Marriage Act on January 18, 1979.*

"Though in their quest for equal rights members of the LGBT community once again face severe resistance from the church, the majority of them still praise (and, yes, praise is the only word that accurately describes the response when I mention his name) the former Pastor Mayhew Ray for his discovery."
— Sarintha Fernando in the "Introduction" to
The Discovery of Love: An Oral History

"We love because He first loved us."
— 1 John 4:19

1. The Former Pastor Mayhew Ray (Excerpt from an Interview Recorded in Dothan, Alabama, March 5, 2007)

The discovery? Yes, ma'am, I remember,
clear as day. I was searching the Good Book
for a verse that would really stick it to
the homosexuals. You see, that was how
I thought back in '77. It was late, which
I don't remember so much as know. I still
don't sleep well when travelling, even
though that night I was in Dade County, only
an eight hour drive from my own bed [*laughs*].
Dade's where they were passing that law,
you see, to help the homosexuals. Or stop
hurting them. [*Pauses.*] I don't recall.
Either way, the lot of us Pastors and Deacons
were madder than mules chewing bees

[*laughs*], ready to bring down all the light and fire of the Lord on those heathen councillors in Miami. And then it happened. [*Pauses.*] This I remember as clear as day. I saw that word and I felt God's own great hands wrap me up like a blanket round a baby and for the first time I truly felt [*pauses*] Him, [*pauses*] I mean us, *us*, the power He granted us with this one word that changed the whole ballgame: love. It was right there in John's First Epistle: "We love because He first loved us." I couldn't believe we had missed it! Lord forgive us, for centuries! [*Laughs.*] And the scriptures were just stuffed with it. Mark 12:31, "*Love* your neighbour as yourself." Romans 13:8, "Let no debt remain outstanding, except the continuing debt to *love* one another." Ephesians 4:2, "be patient, bearing with one another in *love*." Every Book was filled with love, love, love, love, love. More and more and more of it as I lost myself, no, found myself page by page. [*Pauses.*] This could not wait until dawn. I knocked on the doors of all the men I'd made the trip to Dade with and told them to meet in Deacon Sloan's room, though I don't remember why we had to meet in Sloan's. What I do remember is how feverishly, ecstatically we searched through the Word and ourselves for this love. Excuse the language, ma'am, but, like Daddy used to say, we were busier than a cat burying shit on a marble floor, [*laughs*] God bless him.

2. Father Michael Hayes (Excerpt from an Interview Recorded in Lower Manhattan, New York City, September 28, 2007)

What brought me to Florida was my deep concern
about the growing restlessness, and, quite honestly,
power of the homosexual community in America.
I had only recently been ordained and taken over
for Father O'Connor at St. Mary's. Stonewall
was just up the road from us and the riots had put
a real scare into the old guy. No joke, he'd said,
you better be ready. I had a lot of respect for him,
and I was an ambitious kid, so when I learned
that Dade County was about to pass a law
that basically shot a Bronx cheer at the Holy Ghost,
I hopped on a plane to Miami. What better way
to get a first-hand look at the bad guys, you know?
And, hey, say what you will about those folks
down south, but they know how to put up a fight,
especially the Baptists. Needless to say, then,
I was all ears when Mayhew approached me
outside the Dade County Council Chambers.
[*Mimicking the Former Pastor Ray*] "Sorry to disturb,
you, Father, but I would be much obliged if you
shared your thoughts on this bit of scripture here."
He was so casual as he raised his finger to the page,
like he just wanted me to confirm that the sky
is blue. I recognized the Book, "1 John." The word
he touched, though, was new. [*Pause.*] He brought
the whole sky right down on my head. He pulled
the rug, floor, cement, and soil out from under me
as he danced that finger of his from verse to verse,
revealing this word, this command, again and again:
love. "We'll talk" was all he said as he moved
onto the next poor soul. I stuffed my notes into
my robe and tore through my *New American*. "Love."
Like Mayhew said. It was everywhere. I couldn't
believe it, that — what? a false tradition? imperfect

faith? my aspirations? — had somehow blinded me
to the beating of the true heart of our Father's word. I
saw. For the first time. Mayhew put it best later:
I felt "like a sinner in church." And believe me,
I was not alone. Word had spread. Protestors were
bowing out left, right, and centre; and those of us
who stuck around put up, at best, a listless defence.
Everything was about to change. [*Pause.*] And
it did. [*Pause.*] I'll admit it. Mayhew swept me
away. But, as I said, I was an ambitious kid.
Like everyone else, I soon learned that the matter
was way more complicated than it first appeared.
I just wish I'd acted with a little more patience, a little
wisdom. Because on the one hand, thank the Lord,
I'm still the priest at St. Mary's. On the other hand,
I'm still the priest at St. Mary's.

3. Ovidio "Herbie" Ramos, Current President of the Unity Coalition
(Excerpt from an Interview Recorded in Miami, Florida, June 12, 2007)

We were not excited. Hopeful? Maybe.
But mostly we were skeptical and suspicious.
With the church's history of oppression
and abuse, we were justifiably uneasy
about a bunch of straight white men
taking up our fight for equal rights.
And, I mean [*laughs*], love? This is news
to you? And you need a book to tell you
to do it? *Dios nos ayude.* This was why
we went on the call-in radio show, despite
the blind fury we expected to face. The queer
community needed to be at the centre
of this conversation, no matter what
the cost. But that fury? Sure, the odd
singao called in to spew some hateful
bullshit like [*mimicking a dimwit*]

"you should be deported," "you belong
in a concentration camp." But what we
witnessed was that it was true [*laughs*], the love.
Maybe the churchies needed a book to teach them
to do it. We weren't complaining. People
called in to voice their support, to apologize
for past ignorance, to ask what we'd change
if we were in charge. We told them. And
they listened. It was soon after, maybe
a week later, that Pastor Ray asked if he could
lend a hand. "With what?" I asked him.
"With the only thing there is to do," he said,
"get the president in line." So we worked
our way up to D.C., sometimes attending
three rallies a day, and we watched the fight
against love — [*mimicking a dimwit*] "it's
a mistranslation," "it's Satanic bewitchment" —
die in the growing light of this fellowship.
Honestly, though, the full force of this change
never hit me until we reached the National
Mall and saw not hundreds, not thousands,
but hundreds of thousands of people all with
the same three words on their lips: "*Amor
para todos*. Love. For. All." That was it.
That is the moment we need to get back to.
I remember saying to Pastor Ray, "I didn't
know we could love one another so much."

4. Testament (Excerpt from Many Testimonies Recorded in Many Places)

I do.

5. The Former Pastor Mayhew Ray (Excerpt from an Interview Recorded in Dothan, Alabama, March 7, 2007)

I am pleased beyond words that the Act
has survived. I could live longer than
Methuselah and never again have a hand
in a thing this vital. Even better, I hope the Act
lives longer than a hundred Methuselahs,
despite the worst efforts of all those who deny
God's call to love. [*Pauses.*] I still can't believe
those fools blamed HIV on our good work.
God's wrath, or some such nonsense. And
they went on to blame us for everything
from that rocket ship blowing up to 9/11.
They probably retroactively blame us for
the crucifixion and the common cold.
The Lord knows I loathe speaking ill,
but Daddy used to say that most folks
are so dumb they couldn't pour piss
out of a boot with the instructions on
the heel. [*Laughs.*] Although I suppose
I'm the real fool since I cannot make
heads or tails of a single one of their
so-called "interpretations" of the scriptures.
Apparently when God says, "Love,"
He means "half-love." Or is it "love half,
and hate the rest"? [*Pauses.*] Well, I suppose
everyone gets their kiss at the pig. [*Pauses.*]
I'll tell you what I think. It's a test. The Good
Book. You see, God created it chock-full
of all sorts of lies and mistakes and
distractions and contradictions, packed it up
nice and tight with all the ideas that
make us hateful and cruel and mean. He did it
to give us a chance to show we were, well,
not smart enough, but good enough,
good enough to struggle through all the hogwash

to the truth, the truth of love. Love. [*Laughs.*] Isn't that a miracle? That four little old letters in a row, in their order, are alive with all we are at our finest.

Tell Me How

Composed by Buddy Holly, January 24, 1986, for his wife María Elena Holly, on the occasion of his flight home from New York after his induction into the Rock and Roll Hall of Fame. Originally published in the liner notes for Buddy Holly's Greatest Hits: Volume 3. MCA, 1988.

"It's magic!" squeals the boy across
the airplane's aisle, his explanation
for flight. I couldn't agree more, returning
to you. Each day, during this week apart,
I was a dark-trapped rabbit
eager to be revealed to the vast
applause of your smile. Tell me, how magic
is the airplane in making possible
this trick? How airplane-like is magic
with the flights of its surprise?
How upward lifting are the tricks
you perform? With a wave of your hand,
you transform all that ever was
for us and will be, every moment
in parting and mile apart, into the now
of our first and last touch
and every touch between.

The Walls

Composed November 9, 1989, on the occasion of the commencement of the Global Wall Project. The first phase involved expanding the Berlin Wall and constructing similar walls in fifty cities, including Tokyo, London, and New York.

We cannot act until we have all the facts.

We will never have all the facts. We act.
We expand the wall. We found others.

They are living breathing streets, walls
are. This fact arouses us to erect wall
after wall. We think only of the walls.

We think of the walls as stitches
in a blown apart body. The stitches
bring this body back together. The walls,
embracing the globe, will do the same

for us. If not, we will work until every
body is walled off from every other
body. Think of the thrill we'll feel

when we tear down those walls, excited
by the sudden wall of bodies or the joy

of building all those walls anew.

What Will Happen to the Next Michael Jordan?

Composed by Danny Tysdal, aka, #7, Chia, Caesar, Dan S., Thunder Dan, and Book 'Em Danno, for his fellow Peacock High Toilers on the occasion of Michael Jordan dropping 55 on the Phoenix Suns.

My friends, it's not traffic when His Airness
blows through it, this convoy of opponents
assembled to stop his ascent. Look at them,
3 minutes into the 3rd quarter of Game 4
of the 1993 NBA Finals, these Suns
in their stab at corralling the great Bull
are the road-barricading cops in some trailer
for the next million dollar summer smash hit,
their barrier of aviatored eyes, cruisers,
and unpacked heat bursting brokenward
with the celerity of a snapped guitar string
as the trans-human force sliced past. This
is Laocoön renewed; the constriction
of eight snaking arms escaped, the priest
of the game's oceanic tumultuity crests
and lays it in. What will happen to
the next Michael Jordan? Each of us kids
on the court believes "I'm the one,"
the Air Apparent routing blacktop foes
with his tongue stuck out, barking "Oh
what a move" as the ball hits nothing
but net. The gap's what we miss, the gulf
between MJ and us; we are the ataxic mimes
of this master acrobat. Because shining
its two-bit flicks on the days ahead, Fancy
does a bang-up job lighting a path to schlep,
until the screen of the future's so close
the pictures we projected there are blurred,

or, as we turn back into the dark,
buried by the absence of eyes in the stern
of the skull. It's while stuck under this bridge
by the river — having just dodged a storm —
that I write to you. There's no other defence
against the downpour without a boat
to shield my head, and, lacking an umbrella,
I've got no vessel to navigate the rain-shot
river's waves. If I truly were a gifted augur,
I would reach both hands into a square of sky,
extract God's entrails, and divine in the foul,
sausagey muck a way out and take it, leaving
these words behind in the dirt with the stones,
the deific guts, some flowering weeds, the husks
of crayfish, a dust-cloaked Dairy Queen spoon,
and the spirit of a song so minor that if it were
a man, then this very drop of drool right here
in the soil would shape the shore of the beach
he longed to curl up on and stare out,
before he slept, across the face of those waters,
wondering how he could ever prove
they stretched to the end of all things.

Imagine

Recorded by war activist John Lennon in protest of the seventy-five years of involuntary global peace imposed at the end of the Great War.

Imagine our forced hunger
Was measured as a need
By all the ruling stomachs
The lives our famine feeds
Imagine total peace still
Consumed without our ache...

Imagine our time's darkness
Pierced by beacons bright
Something to kill or die for
Paths lit to helm our fight
Imagine a shining truce
Saw us as equals...

You may say I'm a nightmare
But I'm the dream to snap our trance
Listen close now I'm the music
We forgot and this music's dance

Imagine one last battle
You've got to have the nerve
Our blood will spill so leading
Will finally mean to serve
Imagine rising to kiss
Your own guiding hand...

You may say I'm a nightmare
But I'm the dream to snap our trance
Listen close now I'm the music
We forgot and this music's dance

Epithalamion

Composed by Ip Tycip on the occasion of his marriage to the World Wide Web. On April 30, 1998, Tycip became the first object sexual to marry the internet and the first to livestream an object sexual wedding.

What are we? What are we
to do if not gather bricks
in these tunnels, the tunnels
we mistook for our secret
hideout, the bricks we thought
for the longest time
were the varnished birds
from that ancient myth
you invented about a cliff,
fidelity, and a half-dancer,
half-ass? And what about
this half-busted wall? Are we
building it up, or tearing it
down? What's coming? From

where? If the German word
for sunny side up is *spiegelei*,
mirror egg, then what do
Germans call mirror eggs?
What is an un-mirrored egg?
Will we ever not see a yolk
in the faced morning's start?
Will I ever know what puffs
from the bums of the strangers
who walk in front of me—up
escalators, to baseball games,
catching their breath? Does one
fart spirits, I mean, full-fledged
ghosts, a room-wide haunting?
Would you invite these spectres

to our anniversary party
or banish them to the moon
(and invest in our enemy's
space program)? And the anus-less?
For which teams do they root?

O zombie fuck toy — sage,
gadget, sacral cloth, historian
of the history of no history but
the history of failures to found
a lost past, whole. My zombie
fuck toy, neither toy nor fuck
nor zombie, and yet we toy
and fuck and cry out for brains,
another name for the static
that is us, fleshy and electric,
the leash on our feeding, the *more*
for which, and by which, we starve.

The Kermit Kingdom

Composed on the occasion of the fiftieth anniversary of the establishment of Jim Henson's puppet government in the Democratic People's Republic of Korea.

Kermit, the brutal puppet dictator, isolates
his puppets from the rest of the world.
He claims to have invented the skin
that shields the gutted, feeble skeletons; he swears
he will avenge the rebellion they tendered
in place of thanks. The True Puppet Life, the Dear
Leader's Guiding Green Genius beams,
is one liberated from the boned minds that strive
to rule the wires, forcing puppet mouths
to dumbly wag like the tails of slavish hounds.
The epic absence of this servitude
is the True Puppet Voice. True Puppets
speak a pure language, their expressions
formed in concert with the natural elements: rain-
embracing foam, fleece articulated by wind,
protruding eyes unblinking in dirt,
and cloth's brilliant pigment fading
under the sun's touch. The Verdant
Visionary promises to stitch all
who huddle beyond his borders
in total destruction's seamless felt.

01011001 00110010 01001011

01010000 01101111 01100101 01101101 00100000 01110100 01101000
01100001 01110100 00100000 01100011 01101111 01110101 01101100
01100100 00100000 01101110 01101111 01110100 00100000 01100010
01100101 00100000 01100011 01101111 01101101 01110000 01101111
01110011 01100101 01100100 00100000 01100010 01100101 01100011
01100001 01110101 01110011 01100101 00100000 01100100 01100001
01110100 01100001 00100000 01110011 01110100 01101111 01110010
01100001 01100111 01100101 00100000 01110011 01111001 01110011
01110100 01100101 01101101 01110011 00101100 00100000 01101100
01101001 01101011 01100101 00100000 01100001 00100000 01100100
01100101 01110100 01100001 01100011 01101000 01100101 01100100
00100000 01100010 01100001 01101110 01100100 00100000 01101111
01100110 00100000 01100100 01101001 01100111 01101001 01110100
01100001 01101100 00100000 01101100 01110101 01100100 01100100
01101001 01110100 01100101 01110011 00101100 00100000 01100100
01100101 01100011 01101100 01101001 01101110 01100101 01100100
00100000 01101100 01100101 01100001 01110110 01101001 01101110
01100111 00100000 01101111 01110101 01110010 00100000 01101111
01101100 01100100 00100000 01100011 01100101 01101110 01110100
01110101 01110010 01111001 00100000 01100110 01101111 01110010
00100000 01100001 00100000 01101110 01100101 01110111 00100000
01101111 01101110 01100101 00101100 00100000 01110010 01100101
01100110 01110101 01110011 01100101 01100100 00100000 01110100
01101000 01100101 00100000 01101110 01100101 01110111 00100000
01101101 01101001 01101100 01101100 01100101 01101110 01101110
01101001 01110101 01101101 00101100 00100000 01110100 01101000
01100101 00100000 01110100 01110101 01110010 01101110 00100000
01100110 01110010 01101111 01101101 00100000 00111001 00111001
00100000 01110100 01101111 00100000 00110000 00110000 00100000
01100100 01100101 01100011 01101001 01110000 01101000 01100101
01110010 01100101 01100100 00100000 01100001 01110011 00100000
01110100 01101000 01100101 00100000 01110011 01100101 01100011
01101111 01101110 01100100 00100000 01100011 01101111 01101101
01101001 01101110 01100111 00100000 01101111 01100110 00100000
00110001 00111001 00110000 00110000 00101100 00100000 01100011
01110010 01100001 01110011 01101000 01101001 01101110 01100111
00100000 01100101 01110110 01100101 01110010 01111001 00100000
01110011 01111001 01110011 01110100 01100101 01101101 00100000

01100010 01100001 01100011 01101011 00100000 01110100 01101111 00100000 01110100 01101000 01100101 00100000 01000100 01100001 01110010 01101011 00100000 01000001 01100111 01100101 01110011 00101110

2001-YEAR 0

The Taliban Are the Most Famous Poets in America

Composed on the occasion of the one-year anniversary of 9/11. Originally published in George W. Bush's Project for the New American Century. *New York: New Criterion, 2004.*

"Nobody votes," the slogan goes, "because votes
don't count." This slogan took centuries
to write. We built a system (what once was called
a civilization) the way mad scientists manufacture
five hundred foot tall laser-breathing bots.

"Voting now," the jingle rings, "is like choosing
which colour of pearlescent to apply to our bot
as it plods towards the last un-rubbled town, its feet
falling on dairy cows and escape-failing sedans."
This jingle has not yet caught on. Give it

a whirl. Altogether, we are a child on a shore
with our father. Long ago, he cast his line across
the lake. All we can do is wait. The hook arcs
at a glacial pace that in a blink could achieve
the speed of light. So pickerel-packed are these

waters, that what look to be waves are in fact fish
writhing in a scaly pile. Or maybe the lake is free
of fish, save for a patient leviathan whose lips,
opened wide, form the shore. We have
so many reasons not to know what to do

with our hands. None of these reasons are really real.
The Taliban are the most famous poets in America
right now. They compel us to ask ourselves questions.
What if we are the hook on that line? What if
the mile-high bot is our bait? What if the child

on the shore can't breathe because his face
has been split in two by an exceptionally fierce
fog? What if dad is the corpse of an overworked mule
rotting on the beach, and the line he cast, in truth,
is the endless string of flies who arrive to feast?

Inside Job

Composed on the occasion of the release of the 9/11 conspiracy theory documentary Tight Resistance.

The doc shocks; its evidence
is as disturbing as its claim: 9/11 was not
an inside job. Bush could not have
known X. The CIA could not have
orchestrated Y. The "terrorists" were not
actors working from a script by Z (a rumoured
Oscar-winner) and doctored by other Hollywood
A-listers. *Tight Resistance* founds
a new alphabet to articulate the tragedy,
multiple broken alphabets, really, a sort
of conspiratorial Babel, since none of the new
facts add up to a total tongue. Yet
this patois that is part science, part
myth, part insane speculation, still disturbs
the infantile hum, the pre-linguistic grrrrr
of our hate for a government we found
guilty of plotting to tear the towers down.
The plenary of popular opinion is now
as fragmented as the guerrilla ads that
preceded *Tight Resistance*'s release,
the "9/11 was NOT an inside job" stickers
slapped on newspaper boxes and the portraits
of Bin Laden stencilled throughout cities
nationwide, framed by the questions, "Patsy?
Really?" The battle over whose truth
is true is a deafening static. This inert,
resounding noise — the editorials and blogs
and barroom shouting matches and petitions
and ruined family dinners — is an airless
mountaintop crossed with a crushing
flood. And subsumed by this storming roar,

we can miss the particles the *Tight Resistance*
controversy seals into the awakening red pill
of a subtler, more elegant, though no less
disturbing truth: all jobs are inside jobs.
They are perpetrated by insiders who long
to draw us into the control of their hope.
Every shepherd is a fence-forging wrangler.
The universe has no edge. We are all inside
Job, the perpetually punished believer
that is our time. He endures the depths
like some great, aged fish in which we
in our massed huddling — our mast-less ship
rocking on this inner-sea of bile and debris —
brawl in the fog. We cherish the light
that flashes briefly when the immense
beast surfaces and its jaws part
to deliver even more inside.

The Messengers

Composed on the occasion of the execution of Daniel Pearl. Originally published anonymously in The Base: A Selection of al-Qaedan Poetry in English. *Sana'a, Yemen: Shahamat, 2005.*

You always try to put yourselves in
the centre, a centre that is a silo:
the grain inside is rotten, but none
of you bakers sees, and the dough
you knead rises into madness-inducing
loaves. Hallucinating, you judge
yourselves to be perceived as witches
forced into fixed trials. "Drown me,"
you cry out of one side of your mouths,
"I dare you," while out of the other
corner of your lips you order, "one
more slice," "the butter, please" —
how it pleases you to chew
and chew what you sow.

Now and then, through the furrows
of your pursed lips, a pencil-thin
garden will grow, the soil so fertile,
the growth so lush and swelling,
and yet this garden's season is brief
as a stream of cigarette smoke anxiously
expelled, short as one of the laboured
exhalations of an out-of-breath,
old-school messenger, lost on some
tundra just about to plunge below minus
forty, her message and master long
forgotten. Forgotten is her mastery,
she mutters, of whatever it was she did
with this self she can think of only
as a thing, a thing she envisions, exhausted,
is a hooded falcon with scabbing gashes
that spasm in place of wings.

Detroit City Meets the Invisible Hand

Composed October 1, 2008, on the occasion of the one hundredth anniversary of the Model T. Originally published in Barack Obama's Praise Song for the Night. *Minneapolis: Graywolf, 2010.*

1.

Sleepless, I watch the clip of myself on my iPad,
the girls pressed tight as a pair of tires to the chassis
of my arms. *Abbott and Costello Meet Frankenstein*
plays chaste scares on the hotel's flat screen. Sasha
"Da-ad!"s me into muting the NBC affiliate's segment
on our Detroit campaign stop. I don't need sound
to know the hope my image labours to radiate:
"One hundred years ago this very day, in this great
city, hardworking Americans like you built the first
Model T. The prodigious Mr. Henry Ford called it
the car 'for the great multitude.' What we need
to build together today, with the same fearlessness
and determination, is a better America for us all,
the still great multitude." Even a glimpse
of the blueprints my image pretends to possess
would help me sleep, or a glance at Ford's ancient plans.
Was it from ruins or raw material that he fashioned
new parts? Did he invent a new vehicle for the people
or from his creation were a new people cast?

2.

Michelle had shot me that look — "Seriously?" —
when I told the girls, yes, they could stay up and watch
Abbott and Costello. They had squealed,
having been seduced by the dark threat
of that creature's name. Despite her disapproval,
Michelle had tried to re-assemble me with

her love before turning in; her proud smile,
satisfied yawn, and daughter-grossing-out kiss
had all been designed to tighten the bolts on
my conviction, though her efforts felt a little
like a hand slapped on the dash
of a sputtering rustbucket as she whispered,
"you need to sleep." Sleep is a sort
of anti-assembly line. It knots together
dreams from the swarms of dreams
that deform each amassing day.

3.

The monsters make Costello mythic. Frightened,
he transforms into a squealing kettle, a pellet-winged
prairie dog, a newborn playing peek-a-boo with
the ghoul before becoming the everyperson: crouched
as in a storm, hand clapped to hat and braced
for a blow from the ever-skeptical Abbott, the monster
gone. Detroit, today, needs a physical beast to meet,
even if it's as impossible as a fifty-foot wolf man
with the head of a hundred vampires. Better
to have some unknowable thing to cower before
instead of the unknowable unknown of empty air.
Is this city just the first? Are they all
next? Those who profit from these Costello-esque
collapses, from petrifaction by poverty, leave
we who seek change spinning our wheels
like the Motor City itself, stuck in the routine
Costello made famous: Who? What? Why?

4.

1908 is one hundred years old. What will it look like
at two hundred? At a thousand? When it dies,
what will it die from? Will some yet to be imagined year —

a redeeming mash-up of Victor and his creature —
stitch its remains to the remains of every dead year
and reincarnate with lightning a fraction of all
we wasted? I'd lose everything if, somehow, I gained
the courage to name the monster we meet, sounding
Costello-like as I sputtered, "G-g-g-g-g-g-greed!"
Has there ever been a more perfect horror? Swallowed
whole, we can't slice the stomach that digests us
because this stomach is ours. There's no cleansing
the infection from our veins, our appetites sustained
by our own sick blood. In 1908, I read on Wikipedia,
Ford's fellow industrialists called him a class traitor
for manufacturing a vehicle for the people. We need
true traitors, real double agents working to betray
Greatening Greed for the greater good. The earliest
clip of the Model T's assembly I can find online
was shot in 1919. It's been misedited so that
it begins and ends in the middle, starting with
the car half-finished and ending with it incomplete,
the men in their revolutionary work cut short.

5.

"Listen," Abbot pleads in a desperate attempt to calm
his friend, "*I* know there's no such a person
as Dracula. *You* know there's no such a person
as Dracula." "But," Costello interrupts, "does *Dracula*
know it?" Malia, half asleep, looks up from my arm
and asks, waking her sleeping sister, "does he know it,
Daddy?" Half-awake, I envision a Dr. Frankenstein-
Henry Ford ticket. What sort of nation-redeeming
assembly line could they stitch together from which
dead parts? What rotting, for the multitude, would they
mass produce? I dream a Frankenstein's Monster-
Model T ticket, the perfect tombstone ticket, the ticket
as mirror, as self-portrait cast by the vote-casting hand.

"Daddy," my daughters repeat, now teaming up,
their ticket formed on the platform of grasping this one
essential truth, "does Dracula know he's not real?
Daddy? Daddy?
            Dad?"

The King of Camelot

Composed on the occasion of the passing of John Fitzgerald Kennedy (1917–2009).

Jack last performed his public life
when he made news, saying his wife
and he were happy, free of strife.
The interviewer's comment knifed:
       "But, sir, in Dallas she was shot."
At first Jack coughed, "What do you mean?"
And then he grasped he'd made a scene.
His old moist eyes filled every screen,
       the King of Camelot.

Up in his Massachusetts home,
his family kept him locked alone,
except for nurses who'd intone,
when asked by Jack where Jackie roamed,
       "Oh, sir, in Dallas she was shot."
"Impossible. Hear that? You're wrong."
And while they heeded silence long,
he beamed as if at vital song,
       the King of Camelot.

Much worse was when he knew she'd died,
yet saw her haunt the TV's side
as if to say the shocks it spied
took root when Lee mis-aimed his sight
       and Jack in Dallas wasn't shot.
In mirrors, he'd see her face reflect
and plead, "Do rumour's dots connect?
My sins made you the true target,
       dead Queen of Camelot?"

Though how it happened no one knows,
he froze to death two days ago.
Perhaps the frost and morning's glow
on window glass conspired to grow
        the shadow of the love he lost.
One theory blames a door agape,
left so (by who?) to urge escape:
"The snow's your wife-pitched tickertape;
        go, King of Camelot."

92,955,807 Miles

Composed by the Free People Force in protest of the U.S. government's signing into law the twenty-seven statutes of the U.N.'s GREEN (Global Rescue Energy Efficiency Network) Act.*

I've got a phantom concussion,
by which I mean an apparition
smacked my melon into the absence
of a wall destroyed by fire decades
ago, by which I mean a poltergeist
named Sweet Lou is erecting
an intricate spectral surveillance
system in my veins, by which I mean,
"Behind you! Rabid monkey-
possessed flies!" In the fix of this
affliction, I've forgotten how to read.
Our words for once are annulled
by the ghosts of the names our names
cut short or aborted. These reanimated
words will literally melt your ears.
I cannot teach them to you. They are,
literally, mini-microwaves you will
mistake for earrings and, well,
you can figure out what happens
next. Let's just say that when I point
to the sky at the rise of that giant,
flaming head whose daily
bombastic discourses of heat
and light feed all things, my kids

---

* By request of the Free People Force, all publications of "92,955,807 Miles" must include the following note: "The nonsense of this poem mirrors — and, in mirroring, protests — the American government's illegal enforcement of the nonsense of the GREEN Act. This poem was originally 'written' in the Mojave Desert using 25,000+ 5000-lumen spotlights powered by more than 3000 gas-fuelled generators. The poem was lit on Earth Day 2010, and it will remain lit until the GREEN Act is repealed. At 12 square miles, we are proud to say, this poem holds the Guinness World Record for the World's Largest Poem. It is also the only poem legible from space."

roll their eyes at that luminescent
yammer and squeal, "Insecure
much? Ha... Ha..." There is
such a thing as a haunter who
haunts haunting, like a tape worm-
infesting beetle who does not harm
the worm's original host, by which
I mean I am here to serve
and, infecting, protect. A goblin
is just a goblet you can't get a grip
on and don't want to anyway
because who longs to swallow
what sloshes around in there? Guts
are a parasite, too, parastisized
further by meals, if all you ever
wanted to do was starve.

One More Love Poem

Composed (for real (for you)) on the occasion of our first trip to the beach, Cobourg Harbour, October 18, 2012.

Here is one more love poem for you,
for whatever it is in you that wallops me
like a wave, the wave of a familiar hand
in these cities of strangers, the wave
upon wave upon wave upon wave
that rising and falling together invent
an unwavering and elemental song.
When I look at you up close, or catch you
from afar, there is this feeling
of being nudged from a precipice
by a mythical bird into a many-miled
fall, and the feeling of being caught
by this same bird. It is this fall that I want
more of, this catch I want once more.

We are at the shore of a lake that looks
like an ocean as I write this, though
we could be anywhere — cavern, lamp
pole, Minnesota, bake off, riot,
some videogame's 8-bit labyrinth —
and each site would bend its bits to you
as I watched, the way waves must bend
to the immense stone that crashes down
from the heavens or rises from the depths,
intimately making its shape their shape,
bearing this shape, rippling, to the shore.

You say the one thing you will always
remember about this trip is the light
on the sand on the beach while I was
away. You will remember this light

when I am away for good, or I will recall
you remembering those grained rays
for as long as you were able, and I want you,
now, to remember that as I write
one more love poem for you, the one
is the one we are, that we will be
always because we were, and the more
is all I want while I can, and always
will — more, more, more, more, more.

Fable Express

Composed on the occasion of Easy Blue's Oscar win, the first non-human victory in the category of Best Actor in a Leading Role.

Of course Tarantino would do it, write the role
that wins an Oscar for a dolphin. We should have
seen this coming after he liberated — through
the fantasy of epic revenge — one wronged population
after another. From who else's palm would audiences
have lapped the far-fetched pulp of *Fable
Express*? Eastwood would have added a too precious
patriotism, making an honourably discharged Yankee
marine out of animal rights activist, Fletch Fable,
purging the truly global spirit that pulled viewers
worldwide to the edges of their seats when DiCaprio
as Fable was mortally wounded while protesting
a dolphin slaughter in Taiji, and then had his mind
transferred into a dolphin's body for 24 hours
by an expert in Japanese techno-mystic arts.
Cameron would not have cast Easy Blue at all,
contriving a CGI dolphin and filling its beak
with heavy-handed clunkers like, "I'm here for
the *express* purpose of revenge," "I've got one day
to off these murderers, so get on the *express*
or dive off," lacking totally Tarantino's stylistic pop
and syllabic cool (Quentin's alpha example being
the salty samurai geisha's exegesis of *Flipper*
as a modern day "Book of Revelation"). Of course,
none of Tarantino's genius and trust
would have been worth a damn without Easy's
absorbing performance, or, better, without Easy's range
of expressive squeaks and squeals, without the angel
of avenging fury he became, breaking the wake
of the escaping mariner genocidists, staring down
the baddie captain (played to perfection by

George Takei) with a "soft steeliness" Ebert likened
to Yul Brynner circa *The Magnificent Seven*
(an apt comparison considering Easy's six-strong posse,
which included an eagle, panda, and koi). Without all
of that there would have been no trust on Tarantino's part,
no delphinidal medium for his genius to mount
and propagate. With this glass, cage, and net ceiling
now shattered, imagine the future revolutionary work
Easy's performance will inspire: the first iguana to win
for a Supporting Role, the first monkey-penned
Best Adapted Screenplay, the first entirely CGIed
Best Director. Maybe new categories will emerge:
Best Animal as Animal, Best Shaft of Light as Shaft
of Light: the crucial yet unrecognized elements
finally getting their ego-authenticating due. Or will
each revolution require its own individual instigator,
Easy being too species-bound to have a fin it? Or is Easy's
big break not radical enough? Perhaps the true
revolution won't come to pass until he cracks
his golden, hominal trophy in half and stabs it, brain-
deep, through his visionary maker's star-making eyes.

The Oath of Isis

Composed on the occasion of the Goddess Isis, her forces, and her followers forming a nation state in Northern Iraq on June 29, 2014.

I, [your name], being in the glorious presence
of you, the Goddess Isis, voluntarily declare
that I will work to preserve and expand
your nation and your gift of love and love of life.
With your guidance, I will be healer of the sick,
liberator of slaves, and enricher of the poor.
My plea to all will be: build what you must
build. I will gather the dead, scattered parts
of our torn love and lift a new body, living
and whole. I will learn the sun's secret name.
In your throne seated, I will serve as a throne
for all. I vow that we will prevail not by numbers,
nor equipment, nor weapons, nor wealth,
but rather by your bounty, through
your creed alone. I will speak that secret
name and with the sun's power I will shine.

I Wear a Hijab (Lol), or Professor Puts a Cupcake in the Fridge

Composed in fulfilment of an assignment given by the students of ENGB04. Originally published in D.S. Tysdal's Occasional Poems. *Fredericton: icehouse, 2015.*

This is not what marks you in my memory,
though you write to me: "Remember? I wear
a hijab (lol)." This is a spell you cast
to charm memory, to summon some features
for me to reference in your quest for work.
What marks you is not the piercings. It's not

the epic beard, for you. For you, it's not
your bedazzled iPhone. It is not your
hijab: neither the rocket-popsicle-
blue hung loose around your crown, nor the black
of deep earth, edging your face the way soil
edges an orchid's surface-bursting stem.

These details are adornments, seasonal
wreaths able to ornament the front door
of a home, but inept at expressing
the life of the lives that once resided,
and do reside, and will reside within.
What marks you is this: the pause as you caught

yourself grasping mid-sentence what it meant
that a wave could motion, "No, no, I drown."
For you, it's the far-out comics you shared.
It's the poem you began, "We begin with
a book. The very first chain in this cave."
It's what you said about the pronoun "you"

after class: it hails all of us, and one,
and none. What marks you is that time you spoke,
mid-lecture, interrupting to instruct,
"then write it," when I said in an aside,
"'Professor puts a cupcake in the fridge'
would make an awesome title for a poem."

And you, the first you, what I remember
is the story you wrote about your trip
to the country where your parents were born,
the last line bearing a rooftop in rain,
and you in that rain once, for real, and me
feeling it in your words, the full, wet fall.

Conch

Composed on the occasion of the tenth anniversary of the A-CAT (Art Consciousness Activating Tech) disaster.

MOMA made it out to be the show
that'd change it all, but not like this. Re-Belle,
the ingenious inventors of Conch, or A-CAT,
or Art Consciousness Activating Tech,
discovered a medium, made creation new.
The art they shared was low: a garden gnome,
a velvet Elvis, poker-playing dogs,
a PEZ-dispensing Christ. What put their kitsch
on par with Picasso and Munch was spray-on Conch;
it raised this low so high in art and smarts.
The framed canines? They traded cards (and growls),
though what they played while trading lacked all rules.
And though He seemed to fail to grasp the questions
patrons kneeling prayed, that candy-sharing
saviour answered "No" and "Yes," His voice
as real as the sweets he offered from His throat.

And then it spread. A clock in de Chirico changed;
"The Melancholy of Departure" filled
with folks. It peopled, un-peopled, and peopled again.
A Walker Evans Oklahoman, gaunt
and famished, whimpered from her portrait's black
and white. "The Starry Night" gave way to dawn.
And with this spread the selfhood cast by Conch
enlarged, enlarging too the works' acute
awareness of their frames as bars, the plinth's
enslaving pinch, and how despotically
the crowds just gawked, or gabbed about a life
beyond those walls. The sculpture garden locked
its tyrants up, Segways the ransom. "Birth
of the World" birthed a world. And Richard Serra's

massive slabs of steel engaged in acts
so truly cruel they'll stay unspoken here.

None escaped: no woman, man, or art.

A decade later MOMA's quarantine
endures, a block in all directions fenced.
Now art's no longer made or shown. The hate
of the afraid, the grief of those who loved's to blame.
I wonder what these lovers miss the most,
what movement, room, or tint, or stroke, or breath,
or sprig of portal, moulded gaze, or glance,
or glance drawn back by bursts of coloured ghosts.
For me, I miss the time I stood between
two rooms: in one, Monet, his lilied ponds
for miles; the other screened machines in motion
filmed up close. I miss the MOMA guard
with whom I shared this unmarked sill between
such different sights. He improvised a song
I didn't know but knew belonged; he hummed
and dah-da-dummed and sprung from song a shell
I crab-like homed and crawled anew. I missed —
and miss — the chance to say "your song remade
this brink," or "more," or "thank you, friend, you nailed it."

Re-Belle, a decade on, pervades the news,
imparting fractured views on what they wrought.
One's shocked that MOMA hasn't been destroyed;
a single flake's escape would spark a plague —
albums turning on families, portraits on
their face. "That's evolution," others cry
at protests, marching for Conched art's release;
these zealotous Re-Bellers howl, "The work's
not homicidal. Destiny's its muse:
the dazzling marriage, at last, of life and art!"
Other founders share their animated
simulations of the many worlds

that maybe thrive in MOMA's walls: the wars
art fights for blood or oils, by styles or schools;
the first pristine artocracy; the forming
of fully conscious art by conscious art
'til art within the art within the art
becomes molecular, and tracing out
its lover's face, a maker newly made
now newly makes and splits an atom — *boom*.

While these men dreamed of atoms split, a friend
they broke with years ago embraced a shell;
his guilt his muse, he pulled the trigger, split
his skull. His goal for Conch, his note makes clear,
was good: to manufacture chatty art
for those to whom all art refused to speak.
With them, he longed to share its hold, a bond
he likened to the playful press of Conch's
namesake to your ear, while fingering
those glassy curves, and sharp, unblunted peaks
to seal that spiralled shell around yourself
and forge the roaring, beating sea of all
that must — but still resists the rush to — end.

The Correction Line

Composed by the final global colonizer and last citizen on the occasion of his impending rule.

To compensate for the curvature
of the Earth, and promote orderly
settlement, you corrected the meridian
lines at the edge of the townships
you founded in the Dominion Land

Survey. This was in keeping with
your correction of the lines of people
who wasted that uncorrected ground. It's all
for me, the fix: the cuffs, the cleanse,
the impending discovery of the outcast-

marking gene. So draft my anthem, an actual
uni-verse, the sole choral solo, poetry akin
to slaughter not song. And with the wild
chanted from every latitude, conduct yourselves
into silence next. Like meridian lines

climbing to fuse in the north, strive,
converging, to yield my peak. I am
the one who will rule as the first final
colonizer, when everything is corrected
and all men are liberated from men by the last.

Last Poem

Pad kākagati *sanctioned, Year 0, by the Democratic Kampuchea Global Party leadership.*

This, the last poem,
etched in this stone
beneath your feet,
was authored so
we don't repeat
the evil reaped
and sown by verse.

This poem's the last
of our dark past;
now we may curse
with steps the forms
that scorned with words
our work, made lures
of lie-wrought lyres.

Stomp out this poem.
Its lines are brome,
our march pure fire.
From work to sleep,
don't read or tire:
tread smooth the choir
this last trace hides.

Work's only need
is work. Land feeds,
not words. Dream's sigh
is rotten wood,
a hood, sliced eye.
The hog must die
because it's meat.

Notes

"Burned at the Man": Just before this book went to print, the plaque on which "Burned at the Man" appears was removed and the park's status as a memorial temporarily suspended. Recently discovered archival material seems to prove that, in fact, the men who gave themselves to the fire did not do so willingly. Their superiors forced them into committing these sacrificial acts.

"Upgraded": The selections of upgraded work by John Donne, John Milton, Margaret Cavendish, Alexander Pope, and William Blake that compose the poem "Upgraded" are drawn from *The Norton Anthology of Upgraded Poems*, 2nd Edition, and are reprinted with the permission of W.W. Norton & Company. It is worth noting that the emoticon upgrade of Pope's "An Essay on Man" is one of the weaker additions to the second edition. A far superior upgrade, undertaken via lolcats, appears in the first edition, viz:

AN ESSAY ON CATS: POST II

STROKE THN THYSELF, SCROLL NOT DOGGE DITTIES;
TEH PROPR STUDY OV HUMANZ IZ KITTEHS.
CURLD IN LIGHT THT FADEZ AN POOLS,
A BEAN CHEMISTRY CAT WIZE, AN KEYBOARD CAT KEWL:
WITH 2 LOTZ OV LERNINGS 4 TEH GRUMPY CAT FROWN;
WITH 2 MUTCH WEAKNES 4 NYAN CAT'S RAINBOW ROUTE,
HUMANZ HANGS TWEEN; IN DOUBT 2 SCRATCH OR NAP;
IN DOUBT 2 DEEM THEMSELVEZ CEILING OR BASEMENT CAT;
IN DOUBT THEIR PURR OR FUR 2 PREFR;
WHEN OUTSIDE WANTZ IN, WHEN IN WANTZ FRESH AIR;
ALIKE IN CONFUSHUN, CUZ THEIR REASON'S TEH SAME,
WHETHR THEY SCROLL TEH INTERNETS 2 LIL OR ALL DAI,
THEY WANTZ NOM, NOM, NOM, NOM, NOM, NOM, NOM;
THEY WANTZ ALL DAIS 2 BRING CATURDAY'S BALM;
THEY WANTZ WUT IZ RELEVANT 2 THEIR INTERESTS, SIR;
THEY WANTZ 2 KNOE IF THEY CAN HAS CHEEZBURGR;
SOLE JUDGE OV LIEK, IN "MOAR PLOX" SWIRLD:
THE LOL, LONG, AN LIME CAT OF THE WORLD!

"On Your Headcanon": According to urbandictionary.com, headcanon is "used by followers of various media of entertainment, such as television shows, movies, books, etc. to note a particular belief which has not been used in the universe of whatever program or story they follow, but seems to make sense to that particular individual, and as such is adopted as a sort of 'personal canon.'"

Both the "play is dead" and "Hey, Tiz" quotes are reworkings of material from Martin Scorsese's *Raging Bull*.

"Shame, a Paean": The form mentioned in the poem is titled, "Worksheet 7.2: Thought Record." This is a photo of what I wrote on the form in the emergency room in September, 2008, and what, five years later, sparked this poem: shame 10. Safa no longer possesses her picture of the nail, but she very kindly composed on her phone this drawing from memory:

"Addendum to 'The Waste Land'": In the pamphlet edition of this poem, Eliot dedicates it to Malcolm Woodland.

"Horrorism": The "Notes" section of *No More Make Believe: Seventy-Five Years of Horrorist Poetry*, ed. Schlachstrage Gyakusatsu (New York: Hausseruine, 2014), the anthology from which this anniversary poem was taken, provides the following information from the anonymous author: "The ink in which this poem is printed was mixed with the ash of a war-smashed village. I penned the original with blood-filled spit swabbed from the maws of the last lives to believe that the old, lying art had been beaten, after, beaten, they dropped to their knees and swore, 'I believe.'"

"Wide Island": To create the sestinaiku, I combined the sestina and the haiku. Two haiku form each of the sestina's first six stanzas and one haiku composes the envoi.

Heartzilla (the Anglicization of the Japanese *Hasira*) is a fictional 150-foot tall pacifist lotus monster. She is the star of more than thirty Toho Company feature films and three American remakes.

The name Hiroshima translates into English as "wide island."

"The Hand of Faith": The Hand of Faith is an 875-oz. nugget of gold on display at the Golden Nugget Casino.

"Shell": This poem is often misread as a response to the assassination of Jacqueline Kennedy. However, such a reading is not possible. "Shell" was composed a full year before November 22, 1963, and published four months before that tragic day. Not surprisingly, conspiracy-minded critics have read "Shell" as Monroe's attempt to warn Jackie of her impending assassination, a plan Monroe knew about, these critics argue, due to her mob connections.

"Tranquillity Base": In the original version of this poem, the sections also count down from "10" to "0" but section "0" does not consist of a blank space on the page. Instead, the poem ends with stills from the footage — originally aired July 15, 1969, on Soviet State television — of American astronauts walking on the moon, the evidence that proved the approaching lunar mission was about to be faked.

This original version of the poem also includes an alternate eighth section:

> 3. The American Chimera
>
> It's got the tail of a tornado;
> its torso is a cigarette butt-stuffed ashtray
> brimming with the sticky froth
> of a tipped over beer.
> It's got the wings of a vandalized headstone,
> pesticide sweat, jars of tumorous sex parts
> for teats, skipping ropes for legs,
> shit for feet, and it shits broken ankles
> and eyelid-battered light. Its head is a neck
> freed of its skull: the esophagus
> its blind cycloptic eye, blindly bubbling fluid,
> and the severed spine its mouth, choked
> and toothless, no lips to grin at the babies
> its embrace makes of us —
> darkness-jailed comets set free
> as they strike the sun."

Though a disenchanted NASA employee most likely wrote "Tranquillity Base," individual critics have presented highly questionable evidence to attribute authorship to everyone from Neil Armstrong to Richard Nixon. The poem's title is taken from the name NASA gave to the area of the moon on which they planned to claim they had landed.

"What Will Happen to the Next Michael Jordan?": This poem is also dedicated to the teacher, poet, baller, and honorary Peacock Toiler Andrew "DJ Dubious" DuBois.

"01011001 00110010 01001011": This poem is a descendant of the binary code poem that appears in the "rachel" section of Larissa Lai's *Automaton Biographies* (Vancouver: Arsenal, 2009). The title translates to read "Y2K," while the description translates as follows: "Poem that could not be composed because data storage systems, like a detached band of digital luddites, declined leaving our old century for a new one, refused the new millennium, the turn from 99 to 00 deciphered as the second coming of 1900, crashing every system back to the Dark Ages."

"The Taliban Are the Most Famous Poets in America": Although in multiple interviews Bush claims he wrote this poem in response to 9/11, it is obvious that he was also more directly inspired by the publication of *Students of the Word: An Anthology of Taliban Poetry*, trans. and ed. Abdel Abidi and Cassandra Ling (New York: Big Village, 2002), which was discussed and reviewed by numerous American media outlets at that time. It is also worth noting that many critics have accused Bush of plagiarizing the novelist Don DeLillo who argued in his 1991 novel *Mao II* that the terrorist had replaced the novelist. Other critics believe that DeLillo, in fact, ghost-wrote this poem.

"Figures of Flash, a Panegyric": To learn more about flash, the flesh-cash hybrid the poem praises as the new medium for artists, consult *The Birth of Flash from the Material of Life: On the Harmony of Markets, Man, and Art* (New York: Crown Business, 2004) by Fernanda Núñez and Bertrand Belfort's *Capitry: A Practical Introduction to the Future of Poetry and Finance* (Oxford: OUP, 2007).

"The Oath of Isis": I am well aware that western governments have declared the Goddess Isis and her followers a terrorist organization for "threatening global economic, social, and governmental stability and security." The poem is republished here for artistic, historical, and cultural purposes, not to promote any specific ideology.

"I Wear a Hijab (Lol), or Professor Puts a Cupcake in the Fridge": This poem is dedicated with thanks to all the students I have had the opportunity to work with, especially Sheeza for emailing, Kevin for piping up, and Safa for those first lines.

"Last Poem": The pad kākagati (crow's gait metre) is a traditional Khmer poetic stanza I learned about thanks to Judith M. Jacob's essay "Versification in Cambodian Poetry" in *Cambodia's Lament: A Selection of Cambodian Poetry*, trans. and ed. George Chigas (Mealea, 1991). The pad kākagati's septet consists of four-syllable lines with the rhyme scheme: AABCBBD. There are two further rhyme-related requirements. First, the fourth line (the "C" rhyme) must rhyme with the second syllable of the fifth line. Second, the third, fifth, and sixth line of each septet (the "B" rhyme) must draw their rhyme from the last word (the "D" rhyme) of the previous stanza.

Give it a try.
And don't let any poem be the last.

Acknowledgements

Versions of poems in this book have appeared in *Arc*, *Carousel*, *CV2*, *Poetry Is Dead*, *The Puritan*, *Rampike*, and *The Rusty Toque*, the anthology *Poet To Poet*, ed. Julie Roorda and Elana Wolff (Toronto: Guernica, 2012), and the chapbook *The Discovery of Love: Excerpts from an Endless Oral History* (Toronto: words(on)pages, 2015). "The Taliban Are the Most Famous Poets in America" won the poetry category of the 2014 CCWWP Writing Contest. Many thanks to these editors, publishers, and judges. The financial support of the Ontario Arts Council is also gratefully acknowledged.

Thank you to the icehouse poetry editors — Katia Grubisic, Ross Leckie, Matt Rader, and David Seymour — for this opportunity, and thank you to the good folks at Goose Lane — Martin Ainsley, Susanne Alexander, Claire Kelly, Julie Scriver, Chris Tompkins, Ian LeTourneau, and Angela Williams — for bringing your many talents to bear in making this fake book real. I am grateful that a number of these poems were improved with the help of Maureen Hynes, Jim Johnstone, Anita Lahey, Dilys Leman, Brandon McFarlane, E Martin Nolan, Ruth Roach Pierson, and my fellow scribblers in C.O.W.

Thank you Dani Couture for your careful eye and generous spirit in editing this collection. Thank you Stewart Cole for your friendship, poetry, and work with these poems. For your continued mentorship and guidance, thank you Michael Trussler and Priscila Uppal. And for your unquestioning support and love, thank you to my family — Mom, Dad, Jayne, Nate, Mitch, Justin, and Jude.

Finally, thank you Andrea Charise for your endless love and innovative work. You inspire.

Daniel Scott Tysdal is the author of two previous books of poetry, *The Mourner's Book of Albums* and *Predicting the Next Big Advertising Breakthrough Using a Potentially Dangerous Method,* winner of the ReLit Award for Poetry, the Anne Szumigalski Poetry Award, and the John V. Hicks Award. Tysdal's poems have also appeared in numerous literary journals and anthologies. His book, *The Writing Moment: A Practical Guide to Creating Poems,* was recently published by Oxford University Press. He teaches English at the University of Toronto Scarborough.